1st Grade Computer Basics:
The Computer and Its Parts

BABY PROFESSOR

EDUCATION KIDS

Speedy Publishing LLC
40 E. Main St. #1156
Newark, DE 19711
www.speedypublishing.com

A computer is
a machine that
helps us do our
work easier.

The computer
is used in
schools, homes,
and offices.

It helps us write letters and numbers.

THE PARTS OF THE COMPUTER

MOUSE

The mouse's function are pointing, clicking, double clicking, dragging and right-clicking

KEYBOARD

The keyboard has four major parts: alphanumeric, numeric, function and cursor keys.

MONITOR

The monitor looks like a television because you can also see pictures on the screen.

SYSTEM UNIT

The system unit is the brain of the computer. It is called CPU.

PRINTER

There are three kinds of printers: dot matrix, inkjet and laser printer.